WITHDRAWN

NATURE'S MYSTERIES

AURORAS

BEHIND THE NORTHERN AND SOUTHERN LIGHTS

ELISA PETERS

Britannica®
Educational Publishing

IN ASSOCIATION WITH

ROSEN
EDUCATIONAL SERVICES

Published in 2017 by Britannica Educational Publishing (a trademark of Encyclopædia Britannica, Inc.) in association with The Rosen Publishing Group, Inc.
29 East 21st Street, New York, NY 10010

Distributed exclusively by Rosen Publishing.
To see additional Britannica Educational Publishing titles, go to rosenpublishing.com.

First Edition

Britannica Educational Publishing
J.E. Luebering: Executive Director, Core Editorial
Mary Rose McCudden: Editor, Britannica Student Encyclopedia

Rosen Publishing
Shalini Saxena: Editor
Nelson Sá: Art Director
Michael Moy: Designer
Cindy Reiman: Photography Manager
Sherri Jackson: Photo Researcher

Library of Congress Cataloging-in-Publication Data

Names: Peters, Elisa, author.
Title: Auroras : behind the Northern and Southern lights / Elisa Peters.
Description: First edition. | New York : Britannica Educational Publishing,
  in association with Rosen Educational Services, 2017. | 2017 | Series:
  Nature's mysteries | Audience: Grades 1 to 4. | Includes bibliographical
  references and index.
Identifiers: LCCN 2016000286| ISBN 9781680484793 (library bound : alk. paper)
  | ISBN 9781680484861 (pbk. : alk. paper) | ISBN 9781680484557 (6-pack :
  alk. paper)
Subjects: LCSH: Auroras—Juvenile literature. | Geomagnetism—Juvenile
  literature.
Classification: LCC QC971.4 .P48 2017 | DDC 538.768—dc23
LC record available at http://lccn.loc.gov/2016000286

Manufactured in the United States of America

CONTENTS

WHAT ARE AURORAS? 4

BEAUTIFUL FORMS 6

LOOKING FOR AURORAS 8

A GIANT MAGNET 10

EARTH'S MAGNETIC FIELD 14

EARTH'S ATMOSPHERE 18

CAUSING BRIGHT COLORS 20

SOLAR ACTIVITY AND AURORAS 22

UNEARTHLY AURORAS 24

UNDERSTANDING AURORAS 26

GLOSSARY 30

FOR MORE INFORMATION 31

INDEX 32

WHAT ARE AURORAS?

Auroras are beautiful! They are natural displays of colored light that sometimes appear in the night sky. They occur mainly in the northernmost parts of the Northern **Hemisphere** and the southernmost part of the Southern Hemisphere.

Auroras in the Northern Hemisphere are called the northern

Since it is in the Northern Hemisphere, this colorful aurora is the aurora borealis.

lights, or aurora borealis. In the Southern Hemisphere auroras are called the southern lights, or aurora australis. Auroras are named for Aurora, the Roman goddess of the dawn.

Auroras take many shapes and forms, with arcs and rays of colored light being the most common. The light may also look like shimmering curtains, bands, waves, or clouds. An aurora constantly changes shape as the light moves across the sky. The light also may brighten and fade.

These lights over the Australian island of Tasmania are the aurora australis.

BEAUTIFUL FORMS

Auroras often look more clearly defined when they appear closer to Earth's surface. They seem to fade away as they appear farther up in the sky. Different aurora forms have different names. In the corona form, rays seem to meet overhead in a starlike shape. In the flame type, tonguelike rays ripple upward. Verti-

Here you can see the beautiful corona form of an aurora.

THINK ABOUT IT

Look at the aurora photos in this book. Can you think of words of your own to describe the forms you see?

cal rays rising from curving bands are called draperies, which look almost like curtains. The uniform arc is the most stable

form of aurora. It can sometimes last for hours without seeming to change in shape. However, most aurora forms move. Their movement is often described as dancing.

Auroras come in many colors, including red, yellow, green, blue, and violet. However, the most common colors for auroras are light green and pink.

The yellowish-green color of this flame type aurora is the most commonly seen color.

LOOKING FOR AURORAS

Auroras occur throughout the year. However, the best time to see them is in the wintertime. The seasons happen at different times of the year in the Northern and Southern Hemispheres. This is because of the way sunlight falls on different parts of Earth in the course of a year. Ideal months to see auroras in the Northern Hemisphere are from November through February. In the Southern Hemisphere, it is usually best to see auroras during the months of May through August.

The northern lights can be viewed across northern Canada and Alaska,

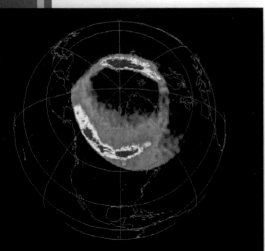

This image shows the areas where the aurora borealis occurs.

Greenland, Scandinavia, and Russia. The southern lights are not often seen because they occur mainly over Antarctica and the southern Indian Ocean. However, some displays might be visible in parts of New Zealand, southern Australia, and the southernmost parts of Chile, Argentina, and South Africa.

Auroras can sometimes be seen outside of the polar regions. In the Northern Hemisphere, they have been seen as far south as 40° latitude. Denver, Colorado, and Philadelphia, Pennsylvania, are both at about 40° latitude.

The oval-shaped zone in which auroras occur is known as the auroral oval. This image shows the aurora australis.

A GIANT MAGNET

A magnet is a rock or a piece of metal that can pull certain types of metal toward itself. You might not guess it, but Earth is a giant magnet! We have Earth's magnetic field to thank for auroras.

Magnetism is a basic force of nature, like electricity and gravity. It happens when tiny particles called

Although it may not look like the magnets you have seen, Earth is a giant magnet, too.

COMPARE AND CONTRAST

Earth's gravity pulls objects down and causes things to fall. How is magnetism like gravity? How is it different?

electrons behave in a certain way. All objects in the universe are made up of tiny atoms. Atoms in turn are made up of electrons and other particles (called neutrons and protons). Electrons have a negative charge, while protons have a positive one. Charge is an amount of electricity related to the balance of electrons and protons in an object. The electrons spin around the atom's nucleus, which contains the other particles. The spinning electrons form tiny magnetic forces. All the tiny magnetic forces from the electrons add up to make the object one big magnet.

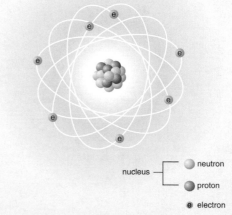

This illustration of a nitrogen atom shows the electrons spinning around the nucleus.

Every magnet has two opposite poles, or ends. These are called a north pole and a south pole. North poles attract the south poles of other magnets, but they repel other north poles. Likewise, south poles attract north poles, but they repel other south poles. The magnetic forces between the two poles of a magnet create a magnetic field. This is the area affected by the magnet.

Like all magnets, Earth has a magnetic field. Earth's north and south magnetic poles are near, but not quite on, its geographic North and South poles. The

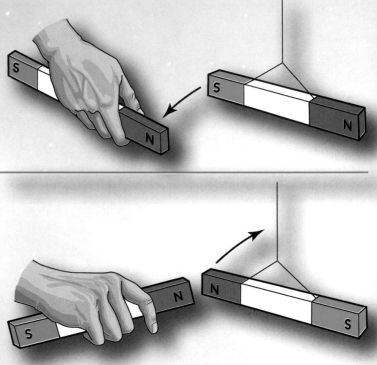

Bar magnets can show how unlike poles attract each other and like poles repel each other.

COMPARE AND CONTRAST

How are Earth's geographic poles and magnetic poles similar? How are they different?

geographic poles are the ends of Earth's axis. The axis is a line around which Earth spins. The planet's magnetic field can be illustrated by lines that connect the magnetic poles. They curve out and around the edges of the field, forming closed loops.

Earth's magnetic field lines line up at its magnetic poles, not its geographic poles.

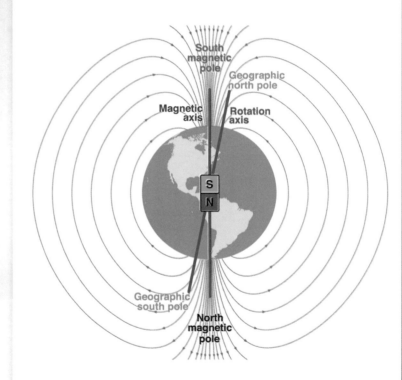

EARTH'S MAGNETIC FIELD

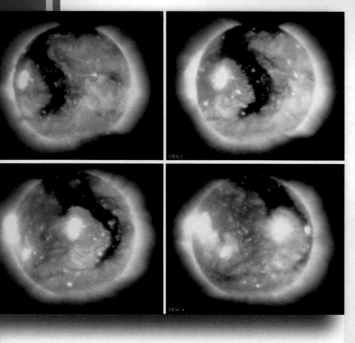

Holes in the Sun's corona, like these, cause strong streams of solar wind.

Scientists believe that huge currents of hot, liquid metal flowing in the planet's **core** create Earth's magnetic field. The field's position occasionally reverses. This means that the north and south magnetic poles switch roughly once every million years.

Earth's magnetic field shields the planet by steering and trapping electrically charged particles, such as the stream of protons and electrons from the Sun. This stream of particles is called solar wind, or solar plasma.

The particles in the solar wind travel at about 1 million miles (1.6 million kilometers) per hour. They reach Earth in a few days. Once trapped, the particles travel in a corkscrew pattern and basically bounce back and forth between the poles. Some particles go into Earth's upper atmosphere. There the particles hit atoms. This causes a glowing display of color to appear in the sky. The display is an aurora!

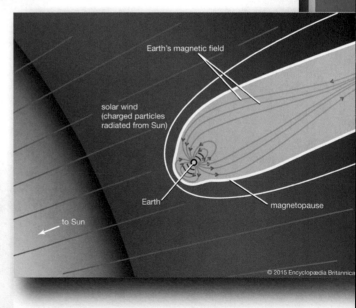

Earth's magnetic field

solar wind
(charged particles
radiated from Sun)

Earth

magnetopause

to Sun

© 2015 Encyclopædia Britannica

It takes about 93 hours for the solar wind to travel from the Sun to Earth.

The region of space in which Earth's magnetic field traps particles from the solar wind is called the magnetosphere. Many of the charged particles remain trapped there. Most of these particles can be found in two regions, called the Van Allen belts. These are located mainly between 5,000 and 20,000 miles (8,000 and 32,000 kilometers) above the ground. In the direction away from the Sun, Earth's magnetic field lines are blown

The colors of auroras are created when particles of the solar wind collide with atoms in the atmosphere.

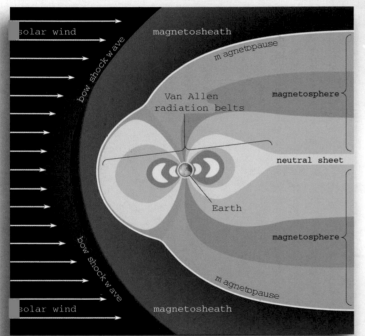

Scientist James Van Allen first detected the Van Allen belts, shown in this diagram, in 1958.

far downwind, reaching over 1 million miles (1.6 million kilometers) into space.

The magnetic field helps protect our planet. It keeps most of the solar wind particles from striking the atmosphere. Without the field, the solar wind might slowly wear away much of the planet's atmosphere.

EARTH'S ATMOSPHERE

The atmosphere is the layer of gas that surrounds Earth. It is often called air. Other planets also have atmospheres. So do some large moons.

Earth's atmosphere is made up of several gases. The gases are held close to Earth by gravity. Near Earth's surface, the atmosphere is about three-fourths nitrogen and one-fifth oxygen. At higher elevations, it is mostly hydrogen and helium.

This illustration shows the five different layers of Earth's atmosphere. Can you see which layer auroras occur in?

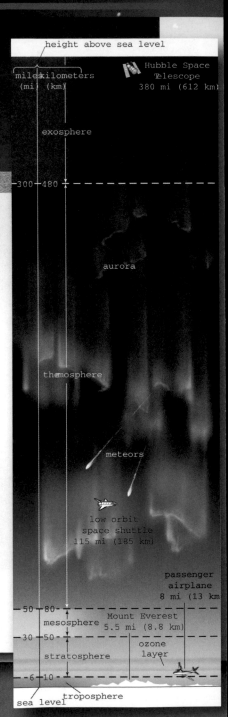

height above sea level

miles (mi) kilometers (km)

Hubble Space Telescope
380 mi (612 km)

exosphere

aurora

thermosphere

meteors

low orbit space shuttle
115 mi (185 km)

passenger airplane
8 mi (13 km)

-300 -480

-50 -80
mesosphere   Mount Everest
5.5 mi (8.8 km)

-30 -50
ozone layer

stratosphere

-6 -10

troposphere
sea level

THINK ABOUT IT

People need oxygen to breathe. Why do you think breathing becomes more difficult for people the farther out (or higher) they travel within Earth's atmosphere?

Scientists divide the atmosphere into five regions, or layers. The layer closest to Earth is the troposphere. The stratosphere is next, then the mesosphere, then the thermosphere, and, finally, the exosphere. Auroras mostly occur in the thermosphere. This layer extends from about 50 to 300 miles (80 to 480 kilometers) above Earth.

Most auroras, such as this curtain of color, occur in the thermosphere.

CAUSING BRIGHT COLORS

Both the green and red in this aurora were caused by solar wind particles colliding with oxygen atoms.

E arth's magnetic field captures charged particles brought by solar winds. There the particles can crash, or collide, with oxygen and nitrogen atoms. This causes the atoms to break up and lose electrons. The atoms become charged, having gained or lost an electron. The ions give off energy called **radiation**. We see this energy as the different colored lights of an aurora.

Green or red light is produced when particles collide with the oxygen in air. Green lights occur at lower heights than red lights. Nitrogen

What kind of collisions do you think caused this aurora over Iceland?

collisions tend to produce blue and purplish light.

SOLAR ACTIVITY AND AURORAS

Magnetic activity within the Sun causes disturbances on the Sun's surface. These disturbances are called solar activity. Solar activity includes sunspots and violent eruptions, such as solar flares and coronal mass ejections (or CMEs). A single CME can contain as much mass as a mountain. Solar activity follows a cycle that takes about 11 years. During a cycle, the

The loop erupting from the right side of the Sun in this photo is a solar flare.

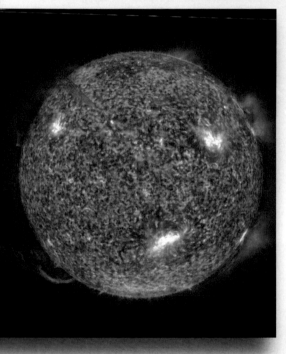

The matter swirling off of the bottom left of the Sun in this image is a CME.

numbers of sunspots and other disturbances increase to a **maximum** and then decrease again. Once each 11-year cycle, the north and south poles of the Sun's magnetic field flip their orientation.

Auroras are more active when there is a lot of solar activity. The increase in activity also increases the chance that an aurora will appear in the sky beyond Earth's polar regions. Like solar activity, aurora activity follows an 11-year cycle.

UNEARTHLY AURORAS

Auroras occur on Jupiter, Saturn, Uranus, and Neptune. These planets all have atmospheres and strong magnetic fields, which are necessary for auroras to occur.

Each planet's aurora looks different. This is because each planet's atmosphere is different. Saturn's auroras produce mainly invis-

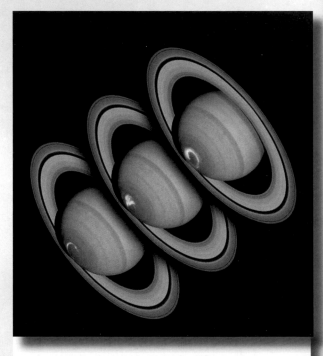

These images of auroras near Saturn's south pole were taken over several days.

ible ultraviolet (UV) light, which can only be seen from Earth with special telescopes. Earth's auroras last for minutes. Saturn's auroras can last for many days.

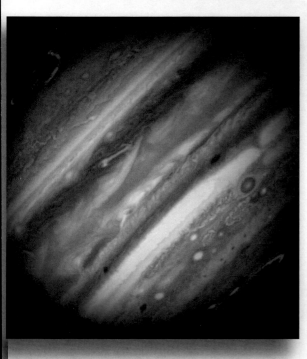

In this image you can see the auroras at both of Jupiter's poles.

Jupiter has huge auroras at its poles that seem to always shine. They are fed by particles from the Sun as well as from Jupiter's moons. Jupiter's moon Io also has auroras. The particles that cause the auroras come from volcanoes on Io. The auroras on Jupiter may be larger than Earth itself.

UNDERSTANDING AURORAS

Denmark's Sophus Tromholt was one of the first scientists to study auroras.

The beautiful and mysterious lights of the auroras have fascinated humans for thousands of years. Descriptions of the lights are found in writings and folklore of many cultures across history. In some traditions the lights were revered as spirits of the dead or as a sign of good news. In other cultures they were feared as a sign of looming disaster.

COMPARE AND CONTRAST

How do you think people's appreciation for auroras has changed over time? How has it stayed the same?

Today people know there are scientific reasons for why auroras happen. However, scientists continue to study auroras to learn more about them. Observatories in Antarctica and the Arctic allow scientists to see auroras and record observations with the latest equipment. Scientists on the International Space Station study auroras from above Earth's atmosphere. Other scientists launch rockets into auroras to study their particles.

Scientists have learned a lot about auroras over the last hundred years.

One reason that people study auroras is because it is a good way to learn about things that affect space weather, such as the solar wind. Space weather can cause big problems for people. It can destroy satellites that are used for wireless communication on Earth, or disturb the signals satellites send. Many things people depend on every day, such as cell phones and navigation systems, rely on satellites. Solar storms may even cause electrical power outages on Earth.

Scientists also study auroras because they are curious

Scientists on the International Space Station took this picture of the aurora borealis.

about them. Perhaps they wonder if auroras occur in other places in the universe. Or perhaps they wonder what specific reasons cause one aurora to look just a bit different from another aurora. Perhaps for some of the same reasons, tourists and scientists continue to go to the coldest areas on Earth to see the glowing, dancing lights.

People visit the Aurora Sky Station in Abisko, Sweden, to experience the aurora borealis for themselves.

ATOMS The small particles that make up all matter.

CHARGE The amount of electricity in a body. A negative charge results from a body having more electrons than protons while a positive charge results from a body having more protons than electrons.

ELECTRONS The particles in atoms that have negative charges.

GEOGRAPHIC POLE The actual north and south pole. Earth's axis of rotation (the line around which it spins) passes through its geographic poles.

MAGNETIC FIELD The area affected by a magnet's pull. It is created by the magnetic forces between the two poles of a magnet.

MAGNETIC POLE One of the two ends of a magnet. Each end of a magnetic is opposite in charge. Earth has two magnetic poles.

MAGNETOSPHERE The area in an atmosphere that is affected by a magnetic field and where charged particles are trapped.

OBSERVATORIES Special buildings with equipment for studying stars, planets, weather, and the sky.

ORIENTATION The way something is faced or directed. Position.

PARTICLES Some of the very small parts of matter (such as molecules, atoms, or electrons).

SATELLITES Machines or natural bodies in space and that move around Earth or another planet.

SOLAR WIND The stream of charged particles from the Sun.

SUNSPOTS Dark spots that appear from time to time on the Sun's surface.

VERTICAL Positioned up and down rather than from side to side.

Books

Bortolotti, Dan. *Auroras: Fire in the Sky*. Richmond Hill, ON: Firefly Books, 2011.

Galat, Joan Marie. *Stories of the Aurora* (Dot To Dot In The Sky). Vancouver, BC: Whitecap Books, 2016.

Hunter, Nick. *Northern Lights* (The Night Sky: and Other Amazing Sights in Space). Chicago, IL: Heinemann-Raintree, 2013.

Rajczak, Kristen. *The Northern Lights* (Nature's Light Show). New York, NY: Gareth Stevens, 2012.

Taylor, Barbara. *DK Eyewitness Books: Arctic and Antarctic*. New York, NY: DK Children, 2012.

Websites

Because of the changing nature of Internet links, Rosen Publishing has developed an online list of websites related to the subject of this book. This site is updated regularly. Please use this link to access this list:

http://www.rosenlinks.com/NMY/aurora

INDEX

Alaska, 8–9
Antarctica, 9, 27
Argentina, 9
atmosphere, 15, 17,
   18–19, 24, 27
atoms, 11, 15, 20
aurora australis, 5
aurora borealis, 4–5
Australia, 9

Canada, 8–9
charge, 11, 14–15, 16, 20
Chile, 9
core, 14, 15
corona form, 6
coronal mass ejections
   (CME), 22

draperies, 6–7

electrons, 10–11, 14–15,
   20
exosphere, 19

flame form, 6

gases, 18
geographic poles, 12–13
Greenland, 8–9

Jupiter, 24, 25

magnetic field, 10, 12, 13,
   14–17, 20, 23, 24
magnetic poles, 12, 13, 14
magnetism, 10, 11
magnetosphere, 16
mesosphere, 19

New Zealand, 9
Northern Hemisphere, 4,
   5, 9

observatories, 27
orientation, 23

radiation, 20–21
Russia, 8–9

satellites, 28
Scandinavia, 8–9
solar flares, 22
solar wind, 15, 16, 17, 20,
   28
South Africa, 9
Southern Hemisphere, 4,
   5, 8
stratosphere, 19
sunspots, 22–23

thermosphere, 19
troposphere, 19